INDIAN LABOUR FORCE:
EMPLOYMENT UNEMPLOYMENT AND SKILL POSITION
(2006)

SUJOY K. SAMANTA
MSC- INTERNATIONAL FINANCE AND ECONOMIC POLOCY
UNIVERSITY OF GLASGOW, UK

Preface

Indian labour force consists of 497 million (2014) members. If it can work to its full potential, it can produce an awesome chunk of the total world output. But to utilize it to its optimum capacity right policy framing is necessary. The country is vast one with varied geography and climate coupled with variety of culture and religious belief. The labour force is also consists of innumerable varieties of skill. A single uniform labour policy is, therefore, not sufficed to utilize the full strength of the entire labour force of the country. Local policies with a central motto to utilize the local resources are the right answers to perform the force in its absolute power.

The book has depicted a scenario of the employment unemployment and skill position of the Indian Labour Force exactly a decade ago. To keep intact the scenario a decade ago in its own position no current data are introduced. Researchers', policy makers will find the book very useful while suggesting or framing policy for the current situation. It is bringing out before them the evolution of the force in changing time.

The author will be grateful to the readers for spending their valuable to time to read the book and also welcome their feedback.

With thanks to the esteemed readers.

The author

The book is dedicated to my wife for her labour and whole hearted support to complete the book and bring it to light.

The author

CHAPTER 1

VARIOUS DEFINITIONS AND THE INDIAN LABOUR FORCE

1.1 Definition of Labour Force, labour force participation rate and unemployment rate

1.2 Indian labour force, the size and the potential

1.3 Production, poverty and productivity of the country

CHAPTER 2

UNEMPLOYNMENT AND EMPLOYMENT PICTURE IN THE COUNTRY

2A. UNEMPLOYNMENT SITUATION

2A.1 Introduction

2A.2 Nature of the unemployment problem

2A.3 Methods of estimation of unemployment:

2A.4 The magnitude and rate of unemployment prevailing in different periods.

2A.5 Unemployment rate among the educated and the uneducated labour force

2A.6 The unemployment position of the country compares to its neighbours.

2A.7 The most recent position of unemployment.

2B. THE EMPLOYMENT SITUATION

2B.1 Structure of employment

2B.2 Growth rate of employment compared to growth rate of labour force and population

2B.3 Output and productivity in the organized and unorganized sectors.

2C Government's special effort to formulate Employment Policy.

2C.1 Task Force On Employment Opportunities.

2C.2 Special Group on Targeting 10 Million Employment Opportunities.

CHAPTER 3

SKILL DEVELOPMENT: VARIOUS ASPECTS.

3.1 Introduction

3.2 The theory of Human Capital

3.3 The present human capital base in India

3.4 The Indian perspective to forming human capital base

3.5 The need for vocational training among the educated and the semi educated.

3.6 The existing vocational systems and the capacity.

3.7 Underutilization of the existing capacity of skill building and redundancy in skills.

3.8 Structural deficiencies.

3.9 Focus of the skill development strategy.

3.10 Government and the private sector's role in skill development.

3.11 Change of outlook of the industry.

3.12 Steps necessary for the informal sector.

3.13 Skill certification procedure.

3.14 Job information in the labour market.

3.15 Counseling and motivating to accept jobs irrespective of sectors.

CHAPTER 4

BUILDING OF CLUSTER: AN EFFECTIVE STRATEGY FOR REDUCTION OF UNEMPLOYMENT AND SKILL DEVELOPMENT.

4.1 Introduction.

4.2 UNIDO's experience in India

4.3 The history and progress in cluster development in India

4.4 Recommendations of the Special Group (2002) on Targeting Ten Million Employment Opportunities per year.

4.5 Job creation in Clusters

4.6 Skill development in Clusters.

4.7 Skill development in rural clusters.

4.8 Some other aspects on cluster development.

Conclusion

CHAPTER 1

VARIOUS DEFINITIONS AND THE INDIAN LABOUR FORCE

1.1 Definition of Labour Force, labour force participation rate and unemployment rate

In economic jargon the commonly used definition of labour force is the group of people who are willing to offer their labour for productive purposes. For estimation and use of data a certain age range, usually from 14-16 to 60-65 is considered to take into account the size of the group. Though according to Tiwari (1996) the age limit for determining economically active population vary in different countries. In his study of 126 countries he observed the following age limits: 6 years and over in Cameroon, Islamic Republic of Iran, Peru, Rwanda and Senegal; 10 years and over in 31 countries; 11 years and over in Thailand; 12 years and over in 12 countries; 14 years and over in 6 countries; 15 years and over in 38 countries; 16 years and over in 10 countries and other age limits in the remaining countries. Whatever be the age limit this group consists of those who are actively working and also those who are seeking work. The category of people who are kept out of this labour force are students, housewives, parents who stay at home, retired people, persons in prison and social institutions, and frustrated workers who are averse to work.

It is seen that within the same age range some people are out of the purview of the labour force. The labour force participation rate is defined as the ratio between the labour force and the total size of the people of the same age range

It is a fact that all members of the labour force are not able to manage offering their labour. The unemployment rate is described as the percentage of the labour force who are not actively engaged in productive work subject to different definition used in this respect.

1.2 Indian **labour force, the size and the potential**

Indian Labour Force is the second largest force in the world in numbers and its size was 375 million in 2002, according to data released by the Government of India on 17th June, 2004. No age limit was mentioned at that figure of labour force. Data released on that occasion also projected an increase to the labour force figure of about 160-170 million by the year 2020. Labour force data released to the press by a private agency[1] on 14th August, 2006 estimate 567 million labour force figure in 2006 at the age group of 20-59 years. They also project a labour force figure of 716 million in 2020. Such a big force is indeed the determinant of world output and may provide new direction to the trend of goods and services produced in the world. But the force is still underutilized. The super capabilities of many of its members are established before the world. This is an indication of its immense potential as a force and latent genius of its members. This force is required to nurture in the proper way to create a human capital stock for the interest not only for the nation but also for the world as a whole.

1. *Source: TeamLease Pvt. Ltd*

1.3 Production, poverty and productivity of the country

The whole world vowed to remove poverty by half of world's 2000 level poverty by 2015, through the resolution adopted in the United Nations in 2000. India is a country which still bears the scourge of poverty, in spite of her being rich in natural and human resources. International Monetary Fund Occasional Paper no. 134 (1995) indicate that steady growth has led to gradual improvements in social indicators, such as , life expectancy, infant mortality, and literacy resulting in the decline in the incidence of poverty, although it remains a serious problem.

The Indian labour force is not producing goods and services to its potential. In support of this statement we have to give a glance of the goods and services production of the country. The country is holding the 12th position in the world ranking of countries in GDP in dollar terms (US$598 billion)[2]. In respect of GDP in PPP terms also the country's position is 4th (US$3096 billion) [3]. After USA, China and Japan. If we compare the labour force of USA and Japan with that of India, except China, then India's labour force is several times more than the two countries. But GDP is few times less. The GDP is less mainly because of two reasons: first, a large proportion is unemployed and second, the productivity of those employed is not equal to the standard of developed countries. Productivity increase of her human resources to the level of industrially developed nations will make her free from poverty and a member of the developed club.

The two problems could be solved by a single prescription of increasing the skill level of the whole labour force.

In writing this book we are concerned to reduce unemployment and underemployment through improvement in the quality of the labour force by development of skills. Therefore, it is imperative that we discuss about the employment and unemployment picture of the country. In the next chapter we shall do that and in the subsequent next two chapters we shall discuss human capital stock, various aspects of skills of the Indian labour force and the alternative strategy to skill development and employment generation; the cluster approach.

2. Source: Pilbeam .K (2006), pp. 145
3. Source: Pilbeam . K (2006), pp. 145

CHAPTER 2

UNEMPLOYNMENT AND EMPLOYMENT PICTURE IN THE COUNTRY

We have divided this chapter into three parts. The first part will cover the unemployment situation in the country. The second part will cover the employment position and in the third part we shall discuss the government's special efforts to formulate the employment strategy in the country.

2A. UNEMPLOYNMENT SITUATION

2A.1 Introduction

Unemployment is a phenomenon occurring not only in India it is a global phenomenon. World Labour Report (2000) indicate that estimated unemployment and underemployment according to World Employment Report 1998-99 were 1 billion at the end of 1998 or one third of the World's Labour Force. It (The World Labour Report 2000) says that the actual number of unemployment people touched 150 million and underemployment between 750 to 900 million and in per cent terms the underemployed were 25 to 30 per cent of the World's workers. The definition of underemployment was people working substantially less than full time, but wishing to work longer, or earning less than a living (World Labour Report 2000). Apprehensions were expressed by the World Labour Report 1997-98 about the bad effects of unemployment in sparking off serious social conflicts in some point of time or other but it felt the consequences in terms of crime, isolationism and marginalization.

Unemployment is a social ill in India for long. Immediate healing of this ill is necessary. We have already prescribed medicine. But description of the situations causing the illness is require at the moment. In describing the unemployment situation of the country it is necessary to take into account the nature of unemployment of the country, method or methods of estimation of unemployment, the prevailing unemployment rate and magnitude of unemployment in different periods, the unemployment rate among the educated and the uneducated labour force, the position of unemployment of the country in comparison to its neighbours and the most recent position of unemployment. The discussion of the above factors will help to grasp the situation thoroughly. We now proceed to discuss all those above factors.

2A.2 Nature of the unemployment problem

The world is divided into two groups: the developed and the developing. India falls in the developing group. Her nature of unemployment is different from the nature of unemployment in industrially developed countries. While narrating the nature of unemployment Dutt and Sundharam (2006) explained it in the following way: The unemployment in the economically advanced countries as Keynes discovered was the deficiency in the effective demand for goods and services. But in India there is prevalence of chronic under-employment or disguised unemployment in the rural sector and there is existence of urban unemployment among the educated class. Therefore, unemployment in India is not the result of deficiency in effective demand but because of the shortage of capital equipments and other complementary resources for production. No doubt this is the right nature of the unemployment in India.

2A.3 Methods of estimation of unemployment:

Estimation of unemployment depends on the definitions of unemployment used for measurement. Planning commission of India is authorized to determine the definition of unemployment. The measurement of unemployment is entrusted to the National Sample Survey Organization (NSSO) which collects data through surveys in Rounds. Three measurements of unemployment are adopted by the National Sample Survey Organization:

(a) Chronic unemployment or 'usual principal status unemployment'. This is measured in number of persons who remain unemployed for a major part of the year. This measurement is more appropriate to those in search of regular employment e. g. the educated and the skilled persons, who may not accept casual work. This is also referred to as 'open unemployment'.

(b) Weekly status unemployment. This is measured in number of persons, who do not find even an hour of work during the survey week.

(c) Daily status unemployment. It is measured in person days or person years, that is, persons who do not find work on a day or some days during the survey week.

2A.4 The magnitude and rate of unemployment prevailing in different periods.

Although unemployment is a serious problem in India. Reliable data on unemployment are available only from 1971.The Committee of experts on Unemployment under the Chairmanship of B. Bhagwati give a picture of unemployment in India in 1971. It reveals from Table 1 that unemployment is a chronic problem that continues from that period. Out of the total labour force of 180.4 million,

18.7 million was unemployed, at a rate of 10.4 per cent. There was difference in rate of unemployment in rural and urban areas. The rural unemployment was 10.9 per cent whereas urban unemployment was 8.1 percent.

Table 1. Unemployment in India, 1971

Category	Total(In millions)	Rural(In millions)	Urban(In millions)
Total number of Unemployed	18.7	16.1	2.6
Total labour force	180.4	148.4	32.0
Total Unemployed as percent of total labour force	10.4	10.9	8.1

(In millions)

Source: Datt and Sundharam, Indian Economy (2006)

Unemployment continues to be a cause of concern for the country is revealed from Table 2, though there is some reduction in unemployment rate compared to 1971. Table 2 gives us the opportunity to compare the unemployment rate in different periods and in different measurements. Rural urban comparison is also possible from table 2. In all the measurements used, rural unemployment rate was lower than urban unemployment rate during the period from 1977-78 to 1999-2000. That was because of the fact that urban labour force was educated more than the rural labour force and there was more unemployment among the educated labour force. In all India average figure there was declining trend in unemployment rate in all categories during 1977-78 to 1993-94 but the trend reversed during 1993-94 to 1999-2000. The reverse trend was due to the reform programme initiated by the country during 1991. The reform programme was initiated in 1991 but it started to produce result from 1993-94. It is clear from Table 2 that during that period (1993-94 to 1999-2000) of reform programs unemployment situation was aggravated.

Table 2: Unemployment Rates: Alternative Measures
(Percentage of Labour Force)

Rural

Year	Usual Principal Status (UPS)	Current Weekly Status (CWS)	Current Daily Status (CDS)
1977-78	3.26	3.74	7.70
1983	1.91	3.88	7.94
1987-88	3.07	4.19	5.25
1993-94	1.80	3.00	5.63
1999-2000	1.96	3.91	7.21

Urban

Year	Usual Principal Status (UPS)	Current Weekly Status (CWS)	Current Daily Status (CDS)
1977-78	8.77	7.86	10.34
1983	6.04	6.81	9.52
1987-88	6.56	7.12	9.36
1993-94	5.21	5.83	7.43
1999-2000	5.23	5.89	7.65

All India

Year	Usual Principal Status (UPS)	Current Weekly Status (CWS)	Current Daily Status (CDS)
1977-78	4.23	4.48	8.18
1983	2.77	4.51	8.28
1987-88	3.77	4.80	6.09
1993-94	2.56	3.63	6.03
1999-2000	2.81	4.41	7.32

Source: Planning Commission, (2001) *Report of Task force on Employment Opportunities*, Table 2.1.

2A.5 Unemployment rate among the educated and the uneducated labour force

Ahluwalia (2001) indicate that the rate of unemployment is typically much higher among the educated than among than among those with lower levels of education.

Table 3: Unemployment* by level of education
(per cent of labour force)

Education Level	Unemployment Rate		
	1987-88	1993-94	1999-00
Non Literate	1.1	0.2	0.2
Literate up to primary	1.9	0.9	1.2
Middle	5.3	3.4	3.3
Secondary	8.7	8.7	5.5
Higher Secondary	-	8.7	7.8
Secondary + Higher Secondary	-	7.1	-
Graduate & Above	9.9	9.3	8.8
Educated (Secondary & Above)	9.0	7.7	7.1
All	**2.7**	**1.9**	**2.2**

* Unemployment rates on usual principle and subsidiary status basis.
Data based on Sample Survey Organization, 43rd Round (1987-88) and 50th Round (1993-94) 55th Round (1999-00)

Source: Planning Commission, (2001) *Report of Task force on Employment Opportunities*, Table 2.8.

Table 3 gives information regarding unemployment rates by education level on usual principal and subsidiary status basis. It is noticed that with the improvement in the level of education unemployment rates also increase. The illiterate and literate up to primary level (four years of school education) do not hesitate to take up any job but there is reservation among the educated in this respect. Educated here means education of secondary level (10 years of school education) and above. The deplorable fact is that unemployment rate among educated in 1999-2000 was more than threefold the unemployment rate of the labour force as a whole. This was because of the fact that the supply of the knowledge they gain was more than the demand for that knowledge. This is another aspect of unemployment which stressed the need for strategy to create quality employment opportunities.

2A.6 The unemployment position of the country compares to its neighbours.

It is pertinent here to mention that in order to assess the degree of unemployment in India a comparison with the incidence of unemployment to its neighbours is necessary. Ahluwalia (2001) mention that there is difficulty in comparison because of differences in definition of methods of measurement used in different countries. The method of measurement used in the countries in Table 4 is on current weekly status basis. In India also current weekly status basis is used. Hence comparison is made on current weekly status basis. On that basis India's unemployment rate is higher than Bangladesh, China, Korea and Malaysia. The unemployment rate is almost at par with Indonesia but lower than Australia, Pakistan, Philippines, and Sri Lanka. If comparison is made on number of unemployment the magnitude is much higher than other countries, except China.

Table 4. Unemployment Rates[@]: India and Selected Countries

Country	Year 1996
India	**4.4**
Australia	8.6
Bangladesh	2.5
China	3.0
Indonesia	4.0
Korea, Republic of	2.0
Malaysia	2.6
Pakistan*	5.4
Philippines	7.4
Sri Lanka	11.3

@ Current Weekly Status Basis
* Figure relates to 1995

$ Pertains to the year 1999-2000 (55th Round, National Sample Survey Organisation)
Source: Planning Commission, (2001) *Report of Task force on Employment Opportunities*, Table 2.2.

2A.7 The most recent position of unemployment.

The National Sample Survey Organization in its 60th Round of Survey on Employment and Unemployment has determined unemployment rates by a sample size. They provide unemployment rate based on current daily status in 2004. For males it was 9.0 percent in 2004, increase from 5.6 percent in1993-94, in rural areas, and in urban areas during the same year it was 8.1 percent, increase from 6.7 percent in 1993-94. The corresponding figures for females was 9.3 percent in 2004, increase from 5.6 percent in 1993-94 in rural areas, and in urban areas it was 11.7 percent increase from 10.5 percent in 1993-94. Overall unemployment rate increased from 7.3 percent in 1993-94 to 9 percent in 2004.

2B. THE EMPLOYMENT SITUATION

To delineate the employment picture of the country it is necessary to discuss the components which form part of the entire scenario. The main components are the structure of the employment, output and productivity of the labour force, growth of employment compared to the growth of labour force and the population. Let us now discuss the components in some detail.

2B.1 Structure of employment

The employment structure of the country is divided into two parts: organized sector employment and unorganized sector employment. It is better we give a brief outline of the above divisions and employment conditions in each of those divisions.

Organized Sector

The organized sector includes all establishments in the public sector irrespective of the number of employees, and non-agricultural establishments in the private sector employing ten or more persons (IMF discussion paper no. 134, 1995). Employment in the organized sector means the work force which is engaged in this sector. Wages in the organized sector are higher than the unorganized sector. The organized sector also provides more job security and other benefits. Public sector jobs within the organized sector give higher wages and related benefits than the private sector for similar jobs which require the same skills.

The share of employment in the organized sector to total employment is declining. This is evident from Table 5. The share of organized sector employment in total employment was 7.93 percent in both 1983 and 1988. This figure declined to 7.08 percent in 1999-2000. In absolute terms, the number was 24 million in 1983, which increased to 27.37 million in 1994 showing a growth rate of 1.20 per cent per annum during 1983-1994. In the post reform period, which is the period after 1991, the growth rate declined to 0.53 percent per annum increasing the employment in absolute terms from 27.37 million in 1994 to 28.22 million in 1999-2000.

The decline in growth was as a consequence of the decline of employment growth in the public sector during 1994-2000, which came down to (-) 0.03 percent per annum. During that period private sector employment grew, from 7.93 million in 1994 to 8.70 million in 1999-2000 at a growth rate of 1.87 percent per annum. In spite of more growth rate in the private sector, growth rate in the organized declined because the public sector accounted for 69 percent of the total employment in the organized sector. It was not possible for the private sector to offset the deceleration in growth in the public sector.

Table 5: Total Employment and Organized Sector Employment

Sector	Employment (million)				Growth Rate (% per annum)	
	1983	1988	1994	1999-00	1983-94	1994-00
1.Total population	718.21	790.00	895.05	1004.10	2.12	1.93
2.Total labour force	308.64	333.49	381.94	406.05	2.05	1.03
3.Total employment	302.75	324.29	374.45	397.00	2.04	0.98
4.Organised sector employment	24.01 (100)	25.71 (100)	27.37 (100)	28.11 (100)	1.20	0.53
5.Public sector	16.46 (68.6)	18.32 (71.3)	19.44 (71.0)	19.41 (69.1)	1.52	(-) 0.03
6.Private sector	7.55 (31.4)	7.39 (28.7)	7.93 (29.0)	8.70 (30.9)	0.45	1.87
7. 4 as % of 3	7.93	7.93	7.30	7.08		
8. 2 as % of	43.0	42.2	42.7	40.4		

Note: 1. Total employment figures are on Usual Status basis
2. The organized sector employment figures are as reported in the Employment Market Information System of Ministry of Labour and pertain to 31st March of 1983, 1994 and 1999.

3. Figures in bracket indicate the percentage of employment in the public sector and private sector to total organized sector employment.

4. Compiled and computed from Planning Commission (2001), Report of the Task Force on Employment Opportunities, p.2.25.

Source: Datt and Sundharam, Indian Economy.

Unorganized sector

There is no clear official definition of the unorganized sector. In general, it is the whole of the economy excluding the organized sector. This sector provides most of the employment to the labour force. Yet it is characterized by low wages, job insecurity and prevalence of low skilled labourers. Table 6 gives a picture of the employment in the unorganized sector for the periods from 1993-94 to 1999-2000.

Table 6: Employment in the unorganized sector

Year	Unorganized sector Employment (millions)	Total employment (millions)	Per cent of employment
1993-94	346.97	374.15	92.2
1999-2000	369.77	397.88	92.9

Source: compiled from Table A of the Planning Commission "Special Group Report of Targeting Ten Million Employment Opportunities"

From Table 6 it is seen that more than 92 per cent of total employment was in the unorganized sector. The importance of this sector in the economy is best described by this figure.

2B.2 Growth rate of employment compared to growth rate of labour force and population

Growth of employment in per cent terms compared to growth of labour force and growth of population in per cent terms gives an overview of the employment situation in the country. We are able to compare all those things from Table 7 for a period of almost three decades. From Table 7 it is clear that growth rate of employment was always falling behind the growth rate of labour force causing unemployment.

Table 7 Rate of growth of Population, Labour Force and Employment

Period	Rate of growth of Population (% per annum)	Rate of growth of Labour Force (Usual principal and subsidiary status) (% per annum)	Rate of growth of Employment (Usual principal and subsidiary status) (% per annum)
1972-73 to 1977-78	2.27	2.94	2.73
1977-78 to 1983	2.19	2.04	2.17
1983 to 1987-88	2.14	1.74	1.54
1987-88 to 1993-94	2.10	2.29	2.43
(1983 to 1993-94)	(2.12)	(2.05)	(2.04)
1993-94 to 1999-2000	1.93	1.03	0.98

Source: Planning Commission, (2001) Report of Task force on Employment Opportunities, Table 2.3.

2B.3 Output and productivity in the organized and unorganized sectors.

Table 8 gives us the clear idea of the supremacy of the unorganized sector in producing output and providing employment. Figures in the table show that around 60 percent of the output was produced in the unorganized sector in all periods from 1993-94 to 1999-2000. Around 90 percent and more of the labour force were employed in this sector compared to 8 percent in the organized sector. But growth rate and labour productivity in the unorganized sector were lower than the organized sector. Supply of Bank credit was also less in this sector. If labour productivity is considered, there is enough scope for expansion of the unorganized sector as labour productivity is almost half of the labour productivity of the organized sector. The expansion of the unorganized sector will produce more output and create more employment opportunities and also remove underemployment.

Table 8: Output and Productivity of the Organized and Unorganized Sectors of the Economy

	Organized Sector			Unorganized Sector	Grand Total
Year/ Growth Rate	Total (1)	Public Sector (2)	Private Sector (3)	(4)	5=1+4
Value added GDP (Rs. in Crores at 1993-94 prices)					
1993-94	256849 (36.8)	180843 (25.9)	76006 (10.9)	441143 (63.2)	697992 (100.0)

1999-2000	418920 (41.1)	266519 (26.1)	152401 (15.0)	600425 (58.9)	1019345 (100.0)
Growth Rate (Per cent)	8.50	6.68	12.30	5.27	6.52
Bank Credit (Rs. 000 Crores)					
1993-94	80.8 (46.0)	28.1 (16.0)	52.7 (30.0)	94.9 (54.0)	175.7 (100.0)
1999-2000	247.4 (62.9)	66.8 (17.0)	180.6 (45.9)	145.9 (37.1)	393.3 (100.0)
Growth Rate (Per cent)	20.5	15.5	22.8	7.4	14.4
Labour productivity growth (percent per annum)	7.88	6.67	8.38	4.10	5.38

Note

1. Figures in brackets are percentages of the grand total in the row

2. Outstanding bank credit refers to all schedules commercial banks

Compiled and computed from the Planning Commission (2002), *Report of Special Group on Targeting Ten Million Employment Opportunities per year.*

Source: Datt and Sundharam, Indian Economy (2006).

2C Government's special effort to formulate Employment Policy.

Some policy initiatives were undertaken by the Central Government during the late 1990s and early 2000s to formulate a strategy for creation of more employment opportunities in the country to solve the problem of unemployment. Two committees were formed to suggest the policy measures to reduce unemployment. They were: Task Force on Employment Opportunities in 1998 and Special Group on Targeting 10 Million Employment Opportunities in 2001. We discuss in brief, the policy measures suggested by the two groups.

2C.1 Task Force On Employment Opportunities.

The Planning Commission of India constitute a Task Force on Employment Opportunities in 1998 headed by Dr. Montek Singh Ahluwalia to go into the detail of the employment and unemployment situation in the country for suggesting measures to create employment opportunities of 100 million people for the next ten years.

Before going to the Task Force report, as a perspective, we discuss briefly the employment target achievement in the Ninth Plan of the country. Ninth Plan (1995-2000) had projected a GDP of 7 percent and employment elasticity (defined as the per cent change in total employment due to one per cent change in GDP growth of the country) of 0.38. The GDP growth rate and employment elasticity failed to reach that target. The actual employment elasticity achieved during 1993-94 to 1999-2000 was 0.15, a dismal failure. The failure was more disappointing in agricultural sector which absorbs 60 per cent of the work force of the country. The employment elasticity in that sector was zero against the projection of 0.50.

The Task Force of the Planning Commission in its report submitted in July 2001 suggested to pursue the failed strategy on employment generation for the next 12 years. The projections of employment generation of the task force report were based on GDP growth.

It projected that 6.5 percent GDP growth will increase the level of employment from 397 million in 1999-2000 to 468 million in 2012 that is an increase of 71 million in a period of 12 years with an annual average growth rate of 5.9 million. With 8 and 9 percent GDP growth rate projection during the same period the Task Force projected employment growth of 84 million and 98 million respectively. The result was that the Task Force failed to provide the right strategies for achieving employment generation of 10 million per year, the sole target for which it was appointed.

2C.2 Special Group on Targeting 10 Million Employment Opportunities.

Following the failure of the Task Force to satisfy the government in the direction of 10 million job creation per year by its recommendations, the Central Government appointed a Special Group Targeting 10 Million Employment Opportunities per year headed by Dr. S. P. Gupta on September 2001.

The Special Group estimated the unemployment level of 26.58 million in 1999-2000 on the basis of National Sample Survey data against 20.13 million in 1993-94 (current daily status basis) as provided in Table 9. The Special Group mentioned that employment elasticity of 0.52 during the 1980s and early 1990s went down to 0.16 in the late 1990s. The employment generation capacity of organized sector came down to near zero and in some cases of the public sector it reached to a negative.

Table 9: Employment and Unemployment in India (1983 to 2000)

Category	1983 (Million persons)	1993-94 (Million persons)	1999-00 (Million persons)	Employment Growth Rate (% per annum)	
				1983-1993-94	1993-94-1999-2000
All India					
1. Population	718.20	894.01	1003.97	2.0	1.95
2. Labour force	261.33	335.97	363.33	2.43	1.31
3. Work force	239.57	315.84	336.75	2.7	1.07
4. No. of unemployed (2-3)	21.76	20.13	26.58	(-).08	4.74
5. Unemployment rate (%)(4÷2*100)	8.33	5.99	7.32		
Rural					
Population	546.61	658.83	727.50	1.79	1.67
Labour force	261.33	255.38	270.39	2.15	0.96

Work force	187.92	241.04	250.	2.40	0.67
No. of unemployed	16.26	14.34	19.50	-1.19	5.26
Unemployment rate (%)	7.96	5.61	7.21		
Urban					
Population	171.59	234.98	276.47	3.04	2.74
Labour force	57.15	80.60	92.95	3.33	2.40
Work force	51.64	74.80	85.84	3.59	2.32
No. of unemployed	5.51	5.80	7.11	0.49	3.45
Unemployment rate (%)	9.64	7.19	7.65		

Source: Planning Commission, (2001) *Report of Special Group on Targeting Ten Million Employment pportunities per year.*

The Special Group stressed the need to boost up unorganized sector which contributed nearly 59 percent of the GDP and 92 percent of the employment in 1999-2000 as given in table 9. Observing the grim unemployment and underemployment situations the Special Group emphasized increase in productivity and job quality in the unorganized sector.

Now we shall move to the next chapter to discuss in detail about human capital stock, various aspects of skills of the Indian labour force and their development strategy.

CHAPTER 3

SKILL DEVELOPMENT: VARIOUS ASPECTS.

3.1 Introduction

Development of skills in the labour force of the country means creation of human capital. Researchers have advocated the creation of human capital base for increasing the productivity and earnings of the labour force. They have measured human capital in terms of years of education spend by a labourer in acquiring knowledge and skills. As human capital content is increased in a labourer his earnings are also increased throughout his life.

A number of factors are involved in forming human capital base of a country. In other words, imparting education and skills to a county's labour force necessitates taking into account a lot of aspects, and those vary from country to country. The aspects involved are, for example, which types of educations are required to impart? Is it general education or technical education? The organizational needs to impart that education. Who are the parties which will take the responsibility to that task(s) and the resources necessary for that task(s) and many other aspects.

In this chapter we shall discuss the general theoretical underpinning of creating human capital base, the present human capital base in India, the Indian perspective to forming human capital base and then, the aspects which are necessary in the Indian context to make the Indian labour force more skilled and productive.

3.2 The theory of Human Capital

The Human Capital theory formulated by Mincer and illustrated by Mazumdar (1989) is reproduced here. In figure 1 the earnings stream over the lifetime of workers due to schooling level Y_0, is represented by the graph AA, where OA is the period of no income while the worker is at school; he then earns a positive amount Y_0, for the entire period of N years of his working life. With a higher level of schooling S, the period of no earnings is extended from OA to OB, but the level of earnings in each year of his working life is higher, as shown by the line BB. The comparison of the two income streams AA and BB is the basis of forming human capital. $Y_s \rangle Y_0$ represents more earnings which is the reflection of more productivity.

Fig 1: Earnings Profiles with Different Levels of Schooling

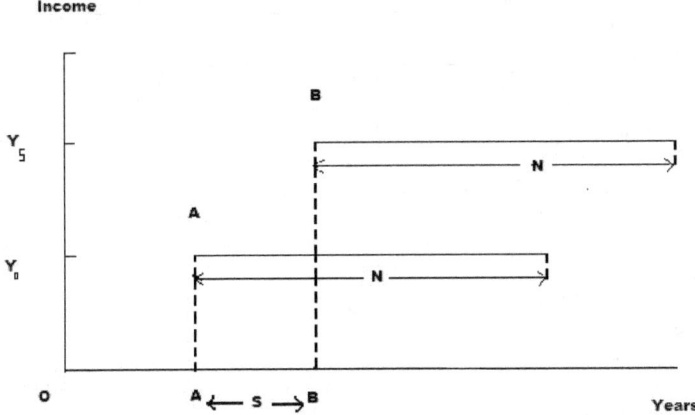

Note: Expected Income at Y_0 with no schooling and at Y_s with S years of schooling, with a work life of N years independent of S.
Behrman and Birdsall (1983)
Source: Mazumdar. D. (1989), Economic Development Institute of The World Bank

While in the Mincer Model the potential worker is require to decide the additional cost of education to reach the Y_s level of income. If the additional cost after proper discounting plus the Y_0 level income is equal to the Y_s level of income, then the worker might have a second thought of incurring that expenditure. But if the additional cost is incurred by the government or the skill accepting industry, then both the parties, the worker and the government or the industry concern are the beneficiaries of the human capital content of the workers. The government is a beneficiary because it will get a return from the labourer in the form of tax revenue and the industry concern is getting the extra efficiency, over and above the wages paid, with which the capital is used by the labourer. This is the theoretical base of the benefit of creating human capital base.

3.3 The present human capital base in India

We can get an idea of the present human capital base in India from the educational profile of the population created by Dutt and Sundharam (2006) from the census of India, 2001 figure which is produced in the Table 10. Table 10 gives that 65.5 per cent of the total population excluding the age group of 0-6 years were literates in 2001. Out of that 3.6 per cent were literate without any educational level. That is they should not be regarded as human capital if years of education is a yardstick for that. 26 per cent had primary school education or four years of school education and 16.1 per cent had middle school education or eight years of school education. The per cent of people of ten years of school education and above was 28.3 per cent.

Table 10: Educational Level in India (2001)

Category	Population (million)	Per cent of total Literates	Literates to total population
1. Total Population	858.2		100.0
2. Illiterates	296.2		34.5
3. Literates	562.0	100.0	65.5
4. Literates without any Educational Level	20.2	3.6	2.4
5. Below Primary	145.0	25.8	16.9
6. Primary	147.0	26.2	17.1
7. Middle	90.5	16.1	10.5
8. Matric/ Higher Secondary	79.4	14.1	9.3
9. Higher Secondary/ But Below Graduate	42.0	7.5	4.9
10. Graduate and above	37.9	6.7	4.4

Note: Population figures relate to population related to age 7 years and above and exclude the age group 0-6. Compiled and computed from Census of India, 2001,C-Series (socio-cultural Tables)

Source: Datt and Sundharam, Indian Economy (2006).

The scientific and technical manpower base is given in Table 11. From the table it is seen that growth of technical manpower during the three decades of 1950, 1960, and 1970 was of the order of more than 10 per cent. That was the period when emphasis was laid on heavy and basic industries. Though growth rate in technical manpower was satisfactory, yet India started from a low reserve base. After the 1970's the growth rate in technical manpower base has decelerated. The total number of projected technical manpower in 2001 was 8434000, which was 1.5 per cent of the total literates at that period. Mathur and Mamgain (2004) refer that low level of human capital content of the work force is the cause of low level of per capita income and incidence of poverty. The above two paragraph suggest a poor reserve of human capital in India.

Table 11: Estimated stock of scientific and technical personnel

					Thousand
Category	1950	1960	1970	1991 (estimated)	2001 (projected)
I.Engineering					
(a) Degree	21.6	62.2	185.4	519.6	1183.

(b) Diploma	31.5	75.0	244.4	859.3	1720.5
II. Medical					
(a) Degree	18.0	41.6	97.8	310.3	415.9
III. Agriculture					
(a) Postgraduate	1.6	3.7	13.5	202.7	285.3
(b) Graduate	6.9	20.2	47.2		
IV. Science					
(a) Postgraduate	16.0	47.7	139.2	482.0	805.0
(b) Graduate	60.0	165.6	42.0	2430.3	4024.9
Total	**155.0**	**415.6**	**1127.3**	**4804.2**	**8434.8**
Growth rate (compound) Over the previous decade		10.4	10.4	7.1	5.8

Computed from data provided by Centre for Monitoring of Indian Economy, Basic Statistics Relating to the Indian Economy, Vol.I, All-India, August 1994 and Indian Applied Manpower Research, Manpower Profile India Year Book, 2004.
Source: Datt and Sundharam, Indian Economy (2006).

3.4 The Indian perspective to forming human capital base

During the development process a nation has to invent and absorb new technologies and produce the productive apparatus for producing the consumer and capital goods to fulfill the needs of the nation. To this end it is necessary that the nation should create such a trained labour force as make efficient use of the modern new technologies. For this purpose, training of the labour force is required in engineering, medicine, management and a lot of other fields. India is on the development process and it lacks human capital as we see in the earlier section. It has opened the economy to attract foreign capital and to increase competitiveness of her industry. Foreign capital will be attracted in a country where the marginal productivity of labour is higher. The neighbouring countries of South East Asian nations and China are progressing rapidly in this direction. If India does not cope with the competition of those countries, foreign capital will operate on those countries and utilize the big consumer market of India. The savings which are at the hands of certain groups of consumers will also be diverted to other countries by their purchasing of foreign goods. If the country succumbs to foreign competition the development process will be hampered. That chance could not be ruled out because from various sources it is worked out that only 5 per cent of the work force of the country is skilled, whereas the skill level of other high growth emerging economies are far above than India. For comparison of the country's skill level a few countries skill level is provided here.

International Comparison Of Skill Level.

Country	Skill Level
South Korea	96 percent
Mexico	20 percent
Botswana	22 percent
Mauritius	36 percent

Source: Gupta (2006) S. P., Globalisation, Economic Reforms and Employment Strategy in India (2006).

The above list gives us the idea that India's skill level is far below the skill level of other high growth developing countries.

Under the above perspective India need to produce a skilled base labour force. The direction is encouraging as Unni and Rani (2004) observed a movement of skilled based work force in the later part of the 1990's.

In the final part of this chapter we now discuss the various aspects which are necessary to make the Indian Labour Force more skilled and productive. The most important aspects, among various aspects, which require some broad discussion are: the need for vocational education among the educated and the semi educated; the existing vocational education systems and the capacity; the focus of the skill development strategy; structural deficiencies; underutilization of the existing capacity of skill building and redundancy in skills; the role of the government and the private sector in skill development; change of outlook of the industry; the steps necessary for the informal sector; uniform skill certification procedure; efficient employment market information system and counseling and motivating to accept jobs irrespective of Sectors. These aspects are discussed in the following sections.

3.5 The need for vocational training among the educated and the semi educated.

The analysis of unemployment situation gives the fact that unemployment among the educated is increasing. This is substantiated by the report of the 'Special Group on Targeting Ten Million Employment Opportunities'. The report shows that out of 26.5 million unemployed in 1999-2000 on daily status basis, the educated unemployed is 10.8 million, or more than 40 per cent of the total unemployed. Of the 10.8 million educated unemployed, the educated youth unemployed number is 8.83 million, that is, 82 per cent of the total educated unemployed. Ahluwalia (2001) mention that this is because of the prejudice in favour of desk jobs or 'white collar' jobs among the educated persons. But we have referred earlier that 'white collar' job opportunities in the public sector is contracting day by day. Sharma, Kumar and Meher (2002) refer the shrinking of job market for the educated workers. This calls for the importance of imparting vocational education among the educated persons, particularly, among the youth to better their job prospect.

Vocational education is also necessary for the educated self-employed. Of the 104-114 million educated and employed workers, nearly 50 to 55 percent are self-employed.

Hence, special vocational training and entrepreneurship development for the self employed need to be developed.

The semi educated youth (up to four years of school education) also need formal and informal vocational training. A large section of this workforce engaged in low productivity and low earning jobs. Their earnings are such that they can not maintain a decent living. To help this sector enter new areas and discover new opportunities, suitable programmes for vocational training and skill development are required. To adjust to their current earnings, process some part time programmes for skill development are also necessary. Those programmes should consider the certification of skills already acquired in informal training. The magnitude of this type of work force is around 60-63 million.

3.6 The existing vocational systems and the capacity.

In India skill acquisitions take place through two basic structural streams - a formal one and a large informal one. The formal structure includes (a) higher technical educational institutions, (Indian Institute of Technology, Engineering colleges etc.) (b) schools providing vocational education to candidates, who have acquired at least ten years of school education (Polytechnic Institutions) and (c) specialized institutions providing technical and apprenticeship training (Craftsman Training, Apprenticeship Training etc). A number of agencies, all are public sector institutions, impart vocational education by their own programmes at various levels. Some of them are short term programmes to augment productivity and to diversify sources to earn supplementary incomes.

The formal channels of the skill development cater only to a small portion of the population. The capacities in the formal institutions are:

Industrial Training Institutes (4700 in number) 630000 positions

Indian Institute of Technology 3000 positions

Engineer Colleges (1200 in number) 350000 positions

Technical Institutions (1220 in number) 230000 positions

Apprenticeship Training Programme 290000 positions

Source: Gupta (2006) S. P., Globalisation, Economic Reforms and Employment Strategy in India (2006)

The total figure comes to something more than 1.5 million. The figure is meagre compared to educated unemployed persons.

In the informal channel skills are acquired by family enterprises and on the job trainings, with no connections to formal institutions, training and certification. Even if the acquired informal skills are high enough to compete with the formally acquired skills they are not recognized in employment in the public or large private sectors. The work force of the unorganized sector have almost no scope for acquiring or upgrading their skills.

3.7 Underutilization of the existing capacity of skill building and redundancy in skills.

So far we discuss the deficiency of skills providing institutions and shortage of skills. But there are also instances of redundant skills and underutilization of the existing capacities. One example is the case in leather industry. In 1995 out of available seats of 420000 in Industrial Training Institutes in leather industry the candidates availed the training were only 635[1]. The social stigma associated with leather related work, absence of modern infrastructure and syllabus may be the cause for low turnout. Another example is the underutilization of vocational education programmes in schools. According to Planning Commission estimate, in 1997-2000 4.8 per cent of 10th level school education pass students attracted to vocational trainings where the capacity was 11.5 percent.

The case for excess production was reported in the trained category. The National Sample Survey Organization in its 55th Round (1999-2000) reported that among the educated unemployed 31 per cent were in possession of professional and technical skills. This was happened because the technical education in graduate engineering was extended relative to diploma level engineering course.

[1]. Source: Gupta (2006) S. P., *Globalisation, Economic Reforms and Employment Strategy in India (2006)*

Another case of lopsided development occurred in technical education is in the case of production of doctors and nurses. While the demand for nurses are growing both in home and abroad, the nursing education is neglected in the country. On the contrary the doctors are relatively more in number than nurses forcing some them to accept low grade employment inferior to their qualification. Ramachandran (2002) find imbalances in the proportion of manpower with different levels of technical competencies.

In the Industrial Training Institutes 80 percent of the total intake capacity is absorbed by 10 top trades and only 20 percent is absorbed by 60 trades.

Gupta (2006) attributed these developments to importance attach by the society to various types of skills, poor learning quality, inadequate labour market information system, inadaptability of training system to changing demand pattern.

3.8 Structural deficiencies.

Training system in the vocational education and training institutions is characterized by structural deficiencies. The vocational training systems were evolved to meet the demand of the organized sector. As long as there is demand in the organized sector for the trained persons, coming out of the vocational education systems, there is no problem. But intake of trained persons into the organized sector is decreasing with the decrease in employment in that sector. This is an indication of changing situation. The vocational institutions should keep pace with this changing situation. They have failed in that direction. They should take in to account the market demand, reorientation of the course curriculum, resource mobilization, coordination among different programmes operating in different parts of the country, quality of training, and flexibility in admission process. But little of these are done.

Training programmes are set in the Industrial Training Institutes without considering the industry need or with out any coordination with the higher technical institutions and informal skill development programmes. Training qualities vary in the ITIs across the country. Entry qualifications are rigid. There is no effort to accommodate the informally trained persons in the ITIs curriculum. There is no alternative source of resources except the government grant. Vocational education programmes in the schools are hampered by absence of quality fulltime teachers, awareness and infrastructures.

Recently some steps has been taken by the Director General of Education and Training to redress the problems of the informal sector by inducing shorter courses of two to six month duration under the Apprenticeship training Scheme and a pilot programme for promoting wage and self employment training.

3.9 Focus of the skill development strategy.

The vocational training system in the country lacks a focused approach. There is no coordination among different department of the governments conducting vocational education programmes. Even the limited resources are not used optimally. There is no standard certification system of the same curriculum conducted in different institutions and not perfectly responsive to labour market demand. Gupta (2006) describe the training system as scattered in nature and lack of a focused approach. The skill development programmes need thorough overhauling to give boost to employment generation and self employment. Forming the nation's youth with such productive skills as meet the demand of the nation. Therefore, the skill development strategy needs a focused approach.

The Special Group has recommended a focused approach that should include: the programmes for development of education and skills for the needs not only for the organized sector but also for the agricultural, small industries and the services sectors; programmes for self-employment in emerging areas like information technology, tourism and financial services; the participation of government, private and nongovernmental organizations; making available of adequate resources for state plans; augmenting facilities for in-service trainings; apprenticeship programme in high tech areas; adoption of training methods by distance learning education system and training of women and non-privileged groups; developing some Industrial Training Institutes as centers of excellence; formation of skilled development fund through partnership between industry and government; multi skilling competency based certification system; quality improvement in management of vocational training system by formation of a National Council of for Vocational Training

The strategies recommended by the Special Group are steps in the right direction which need to implement meticulously.

3.10 Government and the private sector's role in skill development.

Various committees expressed the view that the bulk of the skill development effort should be undertaken by the private sector and the communities. Training provided by the government institutions has not been effectively fulfilled the market demand. The cost of training is very high and efficacy is low. It is therefore, crucial that the users of the skill should make their programmes of skill development and implement according to their requirements. The government should engage itself in administration, coordination, collaboration and evaluation activities but the tasks should be implemented by the industry and the communities. The prowess of the private sector has been shown in the western and southern states, which have generated adequate demand oriented skills through establishment of private Industrial Training Institutes. In the light of this success of the private sector government should consider relieving of its responsibility to running the institutions by itself. But some vocational training should remain in the government's hand. To identify which should remain in the government's control, let us classify vocations in two groups: traditional and modern. In the traditional group, falls the training in the carpentry, plumbing, electrical equipment maintenance etc. Their demands are evenly distributed in the society. The modern group is the upshot of the technological innovation. The trades fall in this group are; the information technology related, medical transcription, biotechnology, advertising etc. The skill building in the second category is mostly undertaken by the private sector and the government has provided the regulatory duties. Those who are getting training from the private sector may have the choice either to wage employment or self-employment in both the formal and in the informal sector. The trainings in the traditional sectors should remain in the governments control because of three reasons; this would help to remain the base of the society strong by creating the knowledge workers at the lower level of the employment market; the traditional sectors will not able to afford the formally trained skilled man power because of their more wage expectations as traditional sectors are characterized by low profit margin, and those who are seeking training in the traditional sectors are ill afford to provide higher cost of training in the private sector because of their low earnings.

3.11 Change of outlook of the industry.

Skill development in the past was viewed by the industry as the duty of the government and remained more or less indifferent in skill building process but was recipient of the benefits of skill building. That outlook is now changing and the industry is coming forward to help in the skill building process. Confederation of Indian Industries (CII) and other industry associations are now involved in dialogue with training institutions. State governments are considering vocational trainings in the industries and are in close interaction with the industry. This interaction process should be making more intensive and extensive. The skill development process should start from the local level. The local communities and industries should assess the need to skills and endeavor to collect resources for establishment of institution at the local level. This type of activity would help match the demand and supply in skills.

3.12 Steps necessary for the informal sector.

We have already discussed that informal sector is a very important sector in employment generation and production of output. A major chunk of the total output comes from this sector. Skill development in this sector will cover a large section of the society with consequent productivity and wage increase. But so far in this sector skill development is not up to the mark, because skill development process was undertaken with an eye to the formal sector. In a globalized environment nobody should be left to become uncompetitive. This sector should be made competitive to resist the pressure of its counterpart in other countries. Where 93 per cent of the labour force is engaged it is needless to say that this sector requires utmost importance. Most of the members of the labour force in the informal sector live in the rural areas and in small towns. It is then essential that training facilities should be extended even to the village level.

3.13 Skill certification procedure.

Uniform certification of skills is essential for testing and comparison. Skills acquired in whichever sectors, that is from formal or informal institutions or self acquired are required testing for judgment of competency, by an authority accepted by all and sundry. Skills acquired in the formal institutions are tested by the institutions themselves. In that case the standard of the testing should be uniform for all the institutions who are imparting the same skills. The informal and self acquired skills are not tested by any authority. These skills should be tested to acknowledge the competency of the workers for their better job prospects. Those who are already in employment should also be given a chance to augment their skills by providing some flexible training systems, such as, part time, distance learning and computerized learning courses. In this regard the certification system of the national body in information technology is a useful model. In that system trainings provided by the private institutions are tested and certified by the Ministry of Information Technology. This should be replicated for other trades also.

3.14 Job information in the labour market.

Workers take trainings either to get a job or to find their preferred job. Employers are also searching for the best worker suitable for them. Therefore, there should be a place where both the parties can fulfill their desire. Such matching will take place only if there is an efficient employment market information system. Not only in information matching, such system should respond to the needs of the employment market by proper modification in training, training capacity and course content.

The Institute of Applied Manpower Research, which currently maintains such information system for professional and technical manpower may give a pioneering role in technical support providing at the local level, coordinating with employment exchanges and other concerned organizations including employers. This should cater to the needs of both formal and informal sector. It is better if this type of system is developed at the local level also.

3.15 Counseling and motivating to accept jobs irrespective of sectors.

The tendency to pursue general education in higher level has been guided by the motivation to acquire secure jobs in the government and public sector and also for social status, (Ahluwalia, 2001). The employment opportunities in the public sector have been reducing day by day. The growing attitude towards technical education has also arisen because of status and more expected lifetime earnings. There is a social stigma in accepting jobs in informal sector or self-employment after pursuing higher education or technical education. In this area effective counseling and necessary motivation is required both from the part of the government and the society, (Gupta,2006).

CHAPTER 4

BUILDING OF CLUSTER: AN EFFECTIVE STRATEGY FOR REDUCTION OF UNEMPLOYMENT AND SKILL DEVELOPMENT.

4.1 Introduction.

Unemployment and underemployment removal is the key to the social welfare. The two help reduction of poverty and increase in productivity and wages. In the earlier chapters we discuss the development of skills of the labour force are the answer to those problems. We also discuss various aspects of skill development. The resources and efforts necessary for skill development of such a huge labour force like India are massive. In the resources front, mobilization of resources, their even distribution and effective utilization are gigantic tasks. Similar is the case in initiation of efforts. Numerous efforts should be initiated from all corners of the society. Cluster development effort is an effort in the direction of both skill development and unemployment reduction

Cluster is defined as the concentration of largely homogeneous enterprises within a limited geographical area which facilitates; fulfilling the similar needs, sharing of fixed cost of infrastructures, mutual support and dissemination of best practices because of the pervasiveness of demonstration effects, (International Labour Organization 2000). The enterprises referred are small scale enterprises. Small scale enterprises (SSE) operating in such clusters derive a clear competitive advantage from:

- The proximity to sources of raw inputs,
- The availability of suitably customized business development services (BDS)
- The abundance of clients attracted by the cluster tradition in the industry, and
- The presence of skilled labour force (International Labour Organization 2000).

Experience in Italy, Germany, USA and Japan describes that small scale enterprises have reached high levels of growth and leadership in profitable niches of world markets (ILO 2000). The cluster approach can combine the benefits of small and medium production units as they are labour intensive and at the same time brings the advantage of large scale operation of technology, marketing, finance, entrepreneurship development and other related aspects.

In this chapter we shall discuss The United Nations Industrial Development Organization's (UNIDO) experience in India in some of the cluster development projects, the history and progress in cluster development in India and the recommendations of the 'Special Group (2002) in Targeting Ten Million Employment Opportunities Per Year'

4.2 UNIDO's experience in India

United Nations Industrial Development Organization started cluster development programmes in four Indian clusters in 1997 considering the crucial role played by the SSE clusters in the country's economy. More than 85 per cent of manufacturing employment is accounted for by small-scale (registered and unregistered) enterprises contributing some 40 per cent of industrial production and 60 per cent of the Indian manufacturing exports are generated by clusters (ILO 2000).

UNIDO cluster in Jaipur

In Jaipur, the capital city of Rajasthan, approximately 550 small firms employing 10,000 workers are engaged in both hand-block and screen printing. During 1980s export demand of those printings picked up heavily. The hand block printers failed to keep up with the growing demand and give way to the screen printers. The hand block printers thus squeeze their profit margin and increase the degree of self exploitation. A study conducted in 1997 identified the unexploited capacity for the traditional artisans in the clusters to target profitable national and world markets. The obstacles the artisans were facing were: the lack of communication among the artisans; the absence of an active association; inadequate quality control capacity of the entrepreneurs; lack of design and marketing skills; inadequate access to credit.

The UNIDO's intervention made possible; the forming of an association, the establishment of a showroom; creation of several networks and an export consortium; introduction of new designs and products; introduction of courses on marketing; establishment of linkages with national and international markets; promotion of a credit scheme; employment of a cluster development agent.

UNIDO cluster in Pune

In the food processing cluster of Pune, the entrepreneurs were facing the stringency of 1954 Food Adulteration Act. The entrepreneurs in absence of adequate skills to comply with the above act were facing obstacles to growth. The UNIDO helped them to acquire the skills necessary to comply with that act and remove the impediments to growth.

The hosiery cluster of Ludhiana

The hosiery cluster of Ludhiana was technologically backward which was hampering their growth. The UNIDO introduce IT skills among the entrepreneurs which they exploit in sharing of ideas and projects through e-mail, procuring information and marketing opportunities through internet.

4.3 The history and progress in cluster development in India

In India cluster based approach started in 1989 targeting the small scale industries by the State Bank of India and subsequently by the Small Industries Bank of India (SIDBI) in 1991.

The government level effort started when the Department of Small Scale Industries (DSSI) of the Ministry of Industry and UNIDO organized a national workshop on "Evolving a Cluster Development Programme" in Mysore, India, to discuss the results of UNIDO cluster activities as well as the experience of other institutions, such as the Small Industries Development Bank of India (SIDBI), the State Bank of India (SBI) and the National Small Industries Corporation (NSIC) and the following recommendations were made (ILO 2000) :

A National Advisory Committee, incorporating the private institutions relevant for cluster promotion activities, will be responsible for the overall coordination of the programme and for defining, together with the DSSI, the resources to be allocated to it. The committee will also be responsible for promoting the exchange of experiences from initiatives undertaken in the different states, and to reorient the services of national institutions when needed.

The states, through their Directors of Industries, will organize a comprehensive assessment of the needs of their clusters, promote the creation of local committees at the cluster level, and support the cluster action plans by providing financial assistance as well as by improving the regulatory framework.

The Local Committees at the cluster level composed of representatives of the private and public sector should play a catalytic role in developing a cluster action plan and in supporting and monitoring its implementation.

In the very next year state governments of various states, various institutions and some nongovernmental organizations also undertake initiatives for cluster based growth of small scale industries

Ministry of Small Scale Industries conducted a survey to derive an estimate of the cluster, registered units and employment in 2003. According to that estimate (Third All India Estimates of Small Scale Industries) there were '1200 Small Scale Industry clusters comprising 280500 registered small scale industry units with employment of 1.38 million persons and estimated output of Rs. 32, 3000 million. The United Nations Industrial Development Organization published a separate list of 388 small and medium enterprises clusters with 490,000 registered small and medium enterprises. Employment and output were to the tune of 7.5 million and Rs. 1570000 million respectively. The estimated cumulative expenditure on cluster development incurred as on 1st January 2004 by various institutions and governments was of the order of Rs. 450 million '[1].

Source: Gupta (2006) S. P., Globalisation, Economic Reforms and Employment Strategy in India (2006),

The cluster development programme is encouraging and slowly increasing its base. About half a dozen state governments have already initiated cluster development programmes and enthusiasm shown by almost all state governments. This enthusiasm need to be materialized in action. For further progress, the step required is to motivate the state governments to acknowledge the cluster development programmes as primary policy to rejuvenating the small scale industries sector and allocate resources for them. To function as net working, data collection, and effective utilization, Local Resource Centre is require to establish at each state. The Local Resource Centre should perform the function of building databases on clusters, training programmes on cluster development personnel, documentation and dissemination of procedures and rapport with similar institution elsewhere.

4.4 Recommendations of the Special Group (2002) on Targeting Ten Million Employment Opportunities per year.

Observing the success of the UNIDO, State Bank of India, Industries Development

Bank of India (SIDBI) and the National Small Industries Corporation (NSIC) in cluster building efforts, the Special Group (2002) realized the role of the clusters in employment creation, building of infrastructures, forming of skills and accordingly, recommended for emphasis on cluster building efforts. The Special Group (2002) identify certain sub-sectors which have a potential for more job creation and skill formation and also mention certain aspects relating to the growth of those clusters. We shall now endeavour to discuss them in the light of the recommendations of the Special Group (2002)

4.5 Job Creation In Clusters

With a view to creating more jobs at an accelerated pace the Special Group (2002) identified the following thrust areas:

- Boosting up of growth in the existing clusters by creating new enterprises and revitalizing the existing ones.

- Classification of clusters in different groups; technology-intensive clusters, labour-intensive clusters, export oriented and skills generation. Importance to those clusters which are labour intensive or have the ability to create more jobs with each unit of capital investment.

- Identify and focus on potentially feasible clusters from amongst the small conglomeration of industrial units which are not yet developed fully as clusters but have a potential and have the capacity to generate more employment.

On the basis of the above thrust areas the Special Group (2002) divided the clusters in the following sub-sectors for employment generation, skill development and growth

Emergent sub-sectors

Some sub-sectors which currently produce relatively small number of jobs but which are likely to grow in the near future and produce more employment. These sub-sectors support the growing export market and there are unutilized or underutilized raw materials and skills. Mainly these sub-sectors are fruit processing, granite processing, agro-services, rural transport, readymade garments, cement ware and small engineering, fish and food processing, silk, minor minerals, rural tourism and leather products locating in different parts of he country.

High growth sub-sectors

These are sub-sectors which register high employment growth rate and skill because of the demand of their products in the domestic and export market. The sub-sectors are silk textiles, fibre products, textile products, cement products, spice processing, freight transport, oil seeds processing, handicrafts, power looms, hosiery, leather products and pottery, situated in various states of the country.

Sub-sectors with high share of employment

There are some sub-sectors which account for a high share of employment in the small and medium sectors. Because they are highly labour intensive. These are; paddy processing, cane processing, fish processing, matches manufacturing, bidi manufacturing, brick manufacturing, cane and wood products, grain milling, gem processing, carpet weaving, wood produces, handloom and pottery.

Service sector clusters

Clusters in the service sectors are very important in the employment generation, skill formation and earnings. Forming clusters in the service sectors initially require some skills. As the clusters are progressing to develop to its potential employment and skill grow side by side. Service clusters also contribute to export growth. Currently service sector contributes most to the Indian economy among the three sectors. Clusters in the service sectors, such as truism, health, food processing, and information technology are the most employment generation and growth potential.

4.6 Skill development in clusters.

Cluster should be regarded as centers for excellence and breeding up of skills. As discussed in earlier chapter skills are developed in the informal sector mainly through two methods: hereditary skills and skills acquired through training on the job. Besides, it is natural that people acquire some skills by demonstration from others and by his own innovation from various works performed. Cluster development will bring all the skills under a single umbrella and act as a skill developing and also skill honing place. Thus cluster development will help skill development in the following way:

- Honing the skill of the persons who entered with some hereditary skills.

- Unskilled will develop skills through instruction and demonstration by other skilled persons.

- Hereditary skilled persons get the opportunity to modify their skills by training from skilled persons from formal institutions who are member of the cluster and vice versa.

- Knowledge related professional skills such as book keeping; official correspondences will spread to other by observation and practice.

- Marketing skills will be developed among most of the persons working in the cluster.

- Clusters are a place where, besides cluster members, people from different background and for different business interests, such as supplier, purchaser, exporter, assemble. Communications and consultation with those people give the cluster members a clear idea of the outside world. Thus their horizon is broadened. That is also a skill which is developed in the clusters.

7 Skill development in rural clusters.

The rural clusters have a high potential in job creation and skill development. The discouraging fact is that there are many obstacles in forming rural clusters and hence rural clusters are not yet developed by the required number. The various obstacles are: people are not fully aware of the job opportunities in the rural clusters; inadequate technical skills and enterprising abilities; the credit availability is limited; problems in marketing the produced products and the bureaucratic non-cooperation and harassment. Provided these obstacles are removed the rural clusters are an important means to income generation, job creation and skill development.

Traditional labour intensive clusters, such as handloom and handicrafts, which can be formed with local resources and skills and clusters, which produce goods that serves the needs of the local market can be formed in the rural areas.

To develop the rural clusters with their full potential intensive entrepreneurship and skill development programme from the part of the government, Non-government organizations and industry are essential.

4.8 Some other aspects on cluster development.

Clusters will be developed by their potential when all the conditions of their development are fulfilled. The most important conditions are credit availability, technology, marketing and export, infrastructure, proper categorization of clusters, selection criteria and the need to involve large industries in the cluster development programmes. Let us now discuss these aspects in the following sections.

Availability of credit

Clusters fulfill their credit needs from both the formal and the informal channels. The formal channel credit or the institutional credit does not take the important role in credit fulfillment of the clusters. Credits from the informal channels, that is from the known circles of friends and relatives of the entrepreneurs, outweigh the credit from financial institutions. The formal or institutional credit to the clusters is low because the credit institutions have not requisite cluster specific knowledge of credit repayment and growth capacity of the clusters. The formal credit institutions sticking to the requirement of collateral in providing credit to the clusters have hindered the growth of the clustered as well as their credit expansion. The principles of mutual guarantee and faith have not been applied in industrial clusters by credit institutions. In the government level, District Credit Plans, which consider the credit need of the districts, ignore the credit requirements of the clusters while making credit plans. Thus, making available of adequate credit to the clusters is an area which requires the attention of the government.

Technology

Industrial clusters use diverse technologies ranging from labour intensive to advanced automated ones. This diversity reflects the number and quality of products and the various types of markets serviced. But the fact is that only a limited number of firms use advance technology. While most of them use labour intensive manual systems. Technology up gradation or innovation is a rare view in industrial clusters.

Rapports with the technical institutions, defence laboratories and research organizations are not existing. The mutual correspondence between the machinery markers and machinery users are very helpful in up gradation and innovation of machinery and technology. In absence of those, copying of old technology is the practice in industrial clusters. Introduction of suitable technology is another criterion for cluster development.

Marketing and export

Marketing and export require additional skills and knowledge on the part of the entrepreneurs. Natural clusters generally develop from the need of the local market but when the local markets are saturated or occupied by large firms, producing goods at superior technology, entrepreneurs in the clusters feel discouraged. They require to find new market in that situation. But the resources and skills necessary in this effort are not possible for the small entrepreneurs to fulfill. Institutional assistance is required in this field.

Institutional support is also necessary to find market abroad and motivate the entrepreneurs to produce more with support in other associated fields as the UNIDO is doing in some clusters in India, referred in the earlier sections of this chapter. That type of institutional activities is required in all clusters.

Infrastructure

Infrastructures in the cluster development are grouped as general and specific. The general infrastructures are roads, rail networks, ports, power and telecommunications. Infrastructures in the specific category cover facilities for designing, testing, training, research and development, effluent treatment etc. It is deplorable that over the past two decades very few new centers have developed to meet the infrastructure requirements of the clusters. Set up and management of these centers are exclusively done by the public sector. The public-private partnership is not yet developed. Improved services in this area for boosting up of cluster development are considered a priority area. Invention and adoption of new technology by the industry call for up gradation of the facilities to the cluster to keep pace with the requirement of the new industrial age.

Categorizations of clusters

Clusters are existing in various sub-sectors and in large numbers. Out of the innumerable number of clusters, they could be divided into the following broad categories as provided in the table below:

SL. No.	Type of Clusters	Production Relations	Market Relations
1	Artisan Clusters	Local	Local
2	Cottage Industry Clusters	Local	Local/National
3	Ancillary Clusters	Local	National
4	SSI (other than Ancillary) Clusters	Local/National	Local/National
5	Export-oriented	Local/National	Local/International

They will be so divided to make them globally competitive clusters, so that their market crossed the national boundaries.

Selection criteria for clusters

The objectives of cluster development are the generation of more employment, skill development and economic growth. These are basic objectives for developing any clusters. But clusters will be built on a particular location. The ideal type of cluster which suits the location is to be selected. The other aspects of cluster should be judged carefully considering the realities of the factors influencing the development of the clusters. A detail study and survey of the types of clusters, the agencies which will be associated and its sustenance in view of the changing economic environment must be conducted. A suitable policy for its continuous improvements need to framed at the outset. The state government to be motivated by the following ways:

- Giving the perfect sense of the importance of the cluster development

- Making them recognize that cluster development is an important strategy to rejuvenate the small scale industries sector.

- Creating separate divisions in the secretarial and field offices to frame and implement cluster policies.

- Budget allocations for cluster development.

- Creating data bases and making maps of clusters.

- Training for personnel associated with cluster development

- Dissemination and transmission of good practices.

- Making account of job creation and skill development in old and new clusters.

Need to involve large industries in cluster development programmes

The nature and characteristics of the clusters suggest that large industrial units do not benefit much from involvement in the cluster development programmes. This is because of the fact that financial gains arising from the cluster development initiatives are part with by a large number of small industrial units. But large industrial units can share a part of their production process at a cheap rate by participating in the cluster development programmes. To increase their industrial base, the clusters are primary road making. Besides, large industrial units can join in the role of a catalyst or in the development of networks, consortia and related development initiatives. Thus their participation should be motivated on the following points:

- Spreading and sharing modern manufacturing process to small scale-units.

- Exhibiting themselves as pioneer in adopting new technologies to develop confidence among cluster entrepreneurs to adopt the same.

- Disseminating the knowledge and awareness about the certification of their products.

- Performing a leading role in infrastructure development and also connecting and inducing other intending partners to take part in the execution of infrastructure development.

- Forming partnership in procuring common raw materials to utilize the benefit of economies in large quantity procurement.

- Popularize the brand image of the clusters for their further development and encouragement to more clusters making.

- Establishing vertical network or sub contracting between big and small units within the cluster.

Conclusion

Almost every household send their representation to the labour force of the country. Therefore, skill development of the entire labour force and consequent reduction in unemployment are not tasks to be performed by a single individual, group or institution. These are tasks to be finished by the required efforts from all directions of the society. The required resources to complete those tasks should be contributed and managed by all social partners of the country. In the era of globalization, the foreign assistance is also necessary in some respect or the other. The following are very important for an integrated approach to the solution of this most important socio-economic problem.

Awareness of the society

Every member of the society should be aware of the need to increase the competency of the country for growth and development. The society should not expect that the government through its bureaucratic system will make the labour force efficient, rather every member should strive to increase his/her efficiency and induce others to do the same. This one-to-one and one-to-many interaction and cooperation along with the resources and facilities provide by the government will help to ease the process. Society will be aware only if the society is properly educated, therefore, education is a must for awareness of the society.

Information

Awareness and information are complementary to each other. People will be aware if there is sufficient information and when people are aware they search for information. Information is also a vital means to make the society competent to keep pace with the changing and competitive world. Skill formation is hindered by lack of information also. Advance level skill formation requires time and thus proper planning is necessary at the right stage. Adequate information at each stage is vital to smooth progress. Competent agencies to make the people inform at each stage is therefore mandatory.

Attitude of the labour force and the society

Attitude of the labour force is considered a very important factor in the skill development process. We have discussed earlier that students go for higher academic education for securing public sector jobs, particularly, the government jobs, which are considered most secured, respectable and well paid. But this sector is squeezing day by day. If most of the educated labour force go for a few jobs in the public sector, the competition will be fierce and expect a few the rest will remain unemployed, which is exactly the case in India. This attitude needs change both from the labourer and society's point of view. The importance should be given to the earnings. The labour force should be induced to it and the society should also encourage in that.

Resources

The resource constraints of the family is a bottleneck to the skills acquire process. Having the required talent and desire some are bereft of acquiring skills for want of resources. Frustration develops in this hapless group. Institutional resources will encourage the pupils and their guardians to go for possession of higher skills for better future earnings.

Among many others the above four factors are considered very important for skill development process. To make the labour force of the country efficient and competent to meet the challenge of the 21st century, all social partners should work in harmony to remove all the impediments which stand in the way.

Bibliography

Bhagwati. J. N., Desai. P., *India, Planning for Industrialization and Trade Policies since 1951,* Published on Development For Economic Co-operation And Development, Paris by Oxford University Press

Census of India 2001, Final Population Totals - Urban Agglomerations And Towns, Published by Government of India

Chopra. A., Collyns. C., Hemming. R., Parker. K., Chu. W., Fratzscher. O., Occasional *Paper 134, India: Economic Reform and Growth, Published* by International Monetary Fund, Washington D C, December 1995

Datt. R. and Sundharam. K. P. M., Indian *Economy (2006),* 54th ed. Published by S. Chand & Company Ltd.

Fan. S., Hazell. P., Thorat. S. (1999) *Linkage between Government Spending, Growth and Poverty in Rural India, IFPRI, Research Report 110,* Published by International Food Policy Research Institute

Government of India, *The Economic Census (1998)*

Government of India, *The Economic Census (2005)*

Gupta. S. P., *Globalisation, Economic Reforms and Employment Strategy in India (2006),* Published by Academic Foundation
India Development Report (1997), edited by Parikh. K. S. *Indira Gandhi Institute of Development Research,* Published by Oxford University Press Delhi

India Development Report (1997), edited by Parikh. K. S. *Indira Gandhi Institute of Development Research,* Published by Oxford University Press Delhi

Indian Economic Survey (2005-2006), Published by Government of India, Ministry of Finance, Economic Division

Indian Economic Survey (2005-2006), Published by Government of India, Ministry of Finance, Economic Division

International Labour Conference, 92nd Session, Report VI

International Labour Organization, International Conference 2000, *Cluster Development and BDS Promotion: UNIDO's Experience in India,* Published by International Labour Organisation (ILO)

Labour Bureau, Government of India, *Occupational Wage Surveys*

Labour Bureau, Government of India, *Annual Survey of Industries Scheme*

Mathur., Ashok., Mamgian., Rajendra. P. *Indian Journal of Labour Economics, Oct. - Dec. 2004, v. 47, iss. 4, pp. 655 - 76, Human Capital Stocks, The Level of*

Utilisation and Economic Development in India

Mathur., Ashok., Mamgian., Rajendra. P. *Indian Journal of Labour Economics, Oct. - Dec. 2002, v. 45, iss. 4, pp. 1015 - 46, Technical Skills, Education and Economic Development in India*

Mazumdar, D., (1989), *An EDI Seminar Paper. Number 40., Microeconomics Issues of Labour Markets in Developing Countries, Analysis and Policy Implications,* Published by Economic Development Institute of The Wold Bank

Miles. D., Scott. A. (2005) *MacroEconomics, Understanding The Wealth Of Nations,* 2nd edition. Published by John Wiley & Sons, Ltd.

Ministry of Labour, *Report of The National Commission on Labour (2002), 2nd Labour Commission Report,* vol. I and vol. II

Ministry of Labour and Employment, *Indian Labour Statistics (2004), Indian Labour Bureau , Simla and Chandigar*

Ministry of Labour and Employment, Government of India, *Increase in Employment During 2000 - 2002* , Press Information Bureau, Press Release Wednesday, July 07, 2004

Ministry of Labour and Employment, Government of India, *Raising India's Work Force To International Levels,* Press Information Bureau, Press Release Thursday, May 17, 2004

Ministry of Labour and Employment, Government of India, *Unemployment Rate Among Educated Youth,* Press Information Bureau, Press Release Wednesday, May 17, 2006

Ministry of Small Scale Industries and Agro & Rural Industries (2004), *Third All India Census of Small Scale Industries (2001 - 02),* Government of India

National Sample Survey Organisation (NSSO), *Employment and Unemployment in India (1999 - 2000): Key Results NSS 55th Round,* December 2000

Organisation For Economic Co-Operation And Development (OECD), *Migration and the Labour Market in Asia, Recent Trends And Policies,* Published by OECD

Planning Commission, (2001), *Report of Task force on Employment Opportunities*

Planning Commission, (2002), *Report of Special Group on Targeting Ten Million Employment Opportunities per Year*

Pilbeam. K. (2006) *third ed. International Finance,* Published by Palgrave

Ramachandran, H., *Indian Journal of Labour Economics, Oct. - Dec. 2002, v. 45, iss. 4, pp. 999 - 1014, Education, skills Development and Changing Labour Market*

Sharma, R. K., Satish, Kumar, M., Mehar, Surendra, *Indian Journal of Labour Economics, Oct. - Dec. 2002, v. 45, iss. 4, pp. 1129 - 47, Education, Skills and the Labour Market in a Globalisd World: A Case of India*

Singhvi, L. M., et.al, *Unemployment Problem in India, ed. 1977*, Published by The Institute of Constitutional and Parliamentary Studies, New Delhi

Tiwari, S. G., *Review of Income and Wealth, March 1996, v. 42, iss. 1, pp. 107 - 12, Perceptions, Problems and Methods of Preparing Labour Force Accounts in India*

Unni, Jeemol., Rani., Uma, *Indian Journal of Labour Economics, Oct. - Dec. 2004, v. 47, iss. 4, pp. 683 - 92, Technical Change and Workforce in India: Skill Biased Growth*

Website: www.dget.gov.in, Ministry of Labour and Employment, *Government of India, Directorate General of Employment and Training*

World Labour Report, (2000), *Income security protection in a changing world*, Published by International Labour Office, Geneva

World Labour Report, (1997 - 98), *Industrial Relations, democracy and social stability*, Published by International Labour Office, Geneva

World Labour Report, (1989), *Employment and Labour Incomes Government and its employees Statistical appendix*, Published by International Labour Office, Geneva

www.en.wikipedia.org

www.zeenews.com , *Labour force in India to cross 700 mn by 2020: Survey, India Labour Report* 2006, Released by TeamLease Services Ltd. India, 15th Aug. 2006

www.ingramcontent.com/pod-product-compliance
Lightning Source LLC
Chambersburg PA
CBHW070414190526
45169CB00003B/1246